Kaplan Publishing are constantly findi[ng] ways to make a difference to your stud[ents,] exciting online resources really do offer something different to students looking for exam success.

This book comes with free MyKaplan online resources so that you can study anytime, anywhere. **This free online resource is not sold separately and is included in the price of the book.**

Having purchased this book, you have access to the following online study materials:

CONTENT	AAT	
	Text	Kit
iPaper version of the book	✓	✓
Progress tests with instant answers	✓	
Mock assessments online	✓	✓
Material updates	✓	✓

How to access your online resources

Kaplan Financial students will already have a MyKaplan account and these extra resources will be available to you online. You do not need to register again, as this process was completed when you enrolled. If you are having problems accessing online materials, please ask your course administrator.

If you are already a registered MyKaplan user go to www.MyKaplan.co.uk and log in. Select the 'add a book' feature and enter the ISBN number of this book and the unique pass key at the bottom of this card. Then click 'finished' or 'add another book'. You may add as many books as you have purchased from this screen.

If you purchased through Kaplan Flexible Learning or via the Kaplan Publishing website you will automatically receive an e-mail invitation to MyKaplan. Please register your details using this email to gain access to your content. If you do not receive the e-mail or book content, please contact Kaplan Flexible Learning.

If you are a new user register at www.MyKaplan.co.uk and click on the link contained in the email we sent you to activate your account. Then select the 'add a book' feature, enter the ISBN number of this book and the unique pass key at the bottom of this card. Then click 'finished' or 'add another book'.

Your Code and Information

This code can only be used once for the registration of one book online. This registration and your online content will expire when the final sittings for the examinations covered by this book have taken place. Please allow one hour from the time you submit your book details for us to process your request.

Please scratch the film to access your MyKaplan code.

Please be aware that this code is case-sensitive and you will need to include the dashes within the passcode, but not when entering the ISBN. For further technical support, please visit www.MyKaplan.co.uk

Professional Examinations

AQ2013 Level 2

Work Effectively in Accounting and Finance

REVISION KIT

British Library Cataloguing-in-Publication Data

A catalogue record for this book is available from the British Library.

Published by:

Kaplan Publishing UK

Unit 2 The Business Centre

Molly Millar's Lane

Wokingham

Berkshire

RG41 2QZ

ISBN: 978-1-78415-353-3

Acknowledgements

The past ACCA examination questions are the copyright of the Association of Chartered Certified Accountants. The original answers to the questions from June 1994 onwards were produced by the examiners themselves and have been adapted by Kaplan Publishing.

We are grateful to the Chartered Institute of Management Accountants and the Institute of Chartered Accountants in England and Wales for permission to reproduce past examination questions. The answers have been prepared by Kaplan Publishing.

CONTENTS

Features in this exam kit

In addition to providing a wide ranging bank of real exam style questions, we have also included in this kit:

- Paper specific information and advice on exam technique.

- Our recommended approach to make your revision for this particular subject as effective as possible.

You will find a wealth of other resources to help you with your studies on the AAT website:

www.aat.org.uk/

Quality and accuracy are of the utmost importance to us so if you spot an error in any of our products, please send an email to mykaplanreporting@kaplan.com with full details, or follow the link to the feedback form in MyKaplan.

Our Quality Co-ordinator will work with our technical team to verify the error and take action to ensure it is corrected in future editions.

INDEX TO QUESTIONS AND ANSWERS

PRACTICE QUESTIONS

EXAM TECHNIQUE

- **Do not skip any of the material** in the syllabus.

- **Read each question** *very* carefully.

- **Double-check your answer** before committing yourself to it.

- Answer **every** question – if you do not know an answer to a multiple choice question or True/False question, you don't lose anything by guessing. Think carefully before you **guess**.

- If you are answering a multiple-choice question, **eliminate first those answers that you know are wrong**. Then choose the most appropriate answer from those that are left.

- **Don't panic** if you realise you've answered a question incorrectly. Getting one question wrong will not mean the difference between passing and failing.

Computer-based exams – tips

- Do not attempt a CBA until you have **completed all study material** relating to it.

- On the AAT website there is a CBA demonstration. It is **ESSENTIAL** that you attempt this before your real CBA. You will become familiar with how to move around the CBA screens and the way that questions are formatted, increasing your confidence and speed in the actual exam.

- Be sure you understand how to use the **software** before you start the exam. If in doubt, ask the assessment centre staff to explain it to you.

- Questions are **displayed on the screen** and answers are entered using keyboard and mouse. At the end of the exam, you are given a certificate showing the result you have achieved.

- In addition to the traditional multiple-choice question type, CBAs will also contain **other types of questions**, such as drag and drop, True/False, pick lists or drop down menus or hybrids of these.

- In some CBAs you will have to type in written answers.

- You need to be sure you **know how to answer questions** of this type before you sit the exam, through practice.

PAPER SPECIFIC INFORMATION

THE EXAM

FORMAT OF THE ASSESSMENT

The assessment has only 1 section which contains 11 tasks and you must complete all them.

The topics for each task are as follows, together with the maximum number of marks that may apply:

Task	Maximum marks	Topics within task range
1	5	Accounting function, policies and procedures
2	8	Reporting lines and contributions of people and functions
3	7	Literacy (email or memo format)
4	8	Prioritisation of work
5	8	Literacy (errors)
6	8	Numeracy
7	6	Personal development
8	8	Literacy (report)
9	6	Impact of work on others
10	8	Ethical principles and behaviour
11	8	Sustainability initiatives and benefits

Time allowed

2 hours

The pass mark for all AAT CBAs is 70%.

Always keep your eye on the clock and make sure you attempt all questions!

DETAILED SYLLABUS

The detailed syllabus and study guide written by the AAT can be found at:

www.aat.org.uk/

KAPLAN'S RECOMMENDED REVISION APPROACH

QUESTION PRACTICE IS THE KEY TO SUCCESS

Success in professional examinations relies upon you acquiring a firm grasp of the required knowledge at the tuition phase. In order to be able to do the questions, knowledge is essential.

However, the difference between success and failure often hinges on your exam technique on the day and making the most of the revision phase of your studies.

The **Kaplan textbook** is the starting point, designed to provide the underpinning knowledge to tackle all questions. However, in the revision phase, poring over text books is not the answer.

The Kaplan workbook helps you consolidate your knowledge and understanding and is a useful tool to check whether you can remember key topic areas.

Kaplan pocket notes are designed to help you quickly revise a topic area, however you then need to practise questions. There is a need to progress to exam style questions as soon as possible, and to tie your exam technique and technical knowledge together.

The importance of question practice cannot be over-emphasised.

The recommended approach below is designed by expert tutors in the field, in conjunction with their knowledge of the examiner and the specimen assessment.

You need to practise as many questions as possible in the time you have left.

OUR AIM

Our aim is to get you to the stage where you can attempt exam questions confidently, to time, in a closed book environment, with no supplementary help (i.e. to simulate the real examination experience).

Practising your exam technique is also vitally important for you to assess your progress and identify areas of weakness that may need more attention in the final run up to the examination.

In order to achieve this we recognise that initially you may feel the need to practise some questions with open book help.

Good exam technique is vital.

THE KAPLAN WKAF REVISION PLAN

Stage 1: Assess areas of strengths and weaknesses

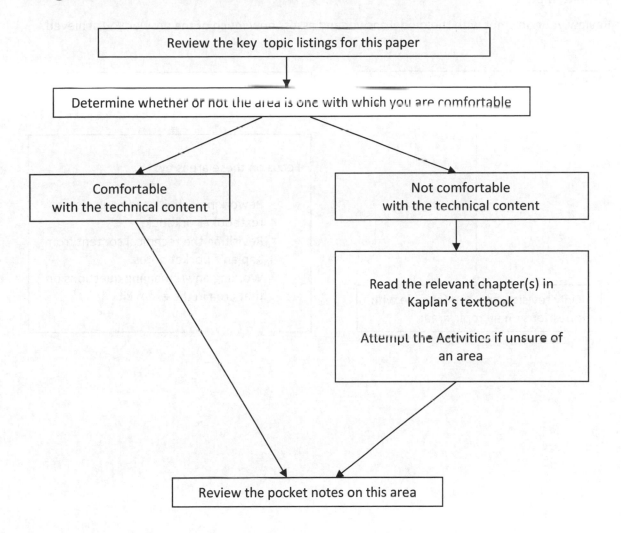

Stage 2: Practice questions

Follow the order of revision of topics as presented in this kit and attempt the questions in the order suggested.

Try to avoid referring to text books and notes and the model answer until you have completed your attempt.

Review your attempt with the model answer and assess how much of the answer you achieved.

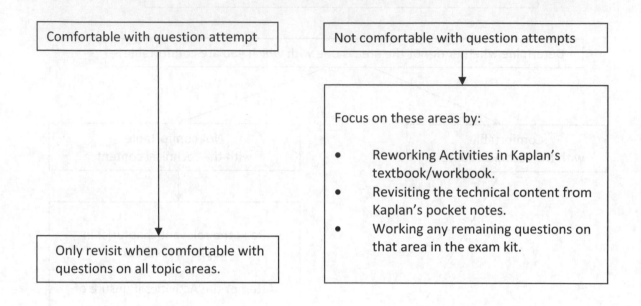

Comfortable with question attempt	Not comfortable with question attempts

Focus on these areas by:

- Reworking Activities in Kaplan's textbook/workbook.
- Revisiting the technical content from Kaplan's pocket notes.
- Working any remaining questions on that area in the exam kit.

Only revisit when comfortable with questions on all topic areas.

Section 1

PRACTICE QUESTIONS

ACCOUNTING FUNCTION, POLICIES AND PROCEDURES

TASK 1

Select three of the following policies and procedures which are likely to apply to the accounting function:

A   Data Protection Act.

B   Health and Safety at Work.

C   Curriculum policy.

D   Authorised signatory procedure.

E   Kitchen Hygiene policy.

F   Administration of substances policy.

TASK 2

Various documents are provided to the accounts department; **match the document to the department sending it:**

Department	*Document*
Purchasing Department	(a) Bank interest charged
	(b) Copy of Purchase order
HR Department	(c) Sales Commission
	(d) New employee forms
Payroll Department	(e) Statutory Sick pay forms
	(f) Customer invoice

TASK 3

Match the following departments to ONE information type

Department	*Information*
Sales Dept	Health and Safety guidelines.
Accounts Dept	List of all new employees for period.
Payroll Dept	Cheque book stubs.
	Commission payable to sales staff.
	Employee car registration numbers.

TASK 4

Select THREE principles from the list below that are not part of the Data Protection Act 1998.

- Data processed fairly and lawfully.
- Information obtained for personal use.
- Historic information that is not up to date.
- Not kept longer than necessary.
- Transferred to other countries without authorisation.

REPORTING LINES AND CONTRIBUTIONS OF PEOPLE AND FUNCTIONS

TASK 5

A business employs 2 Directors, 3 Managers and 6 Assistants. **State who should report to who.**

Sales and Purchase Ledger Assistant	Managing Director
Administration Assistant	Financial Director
3 Sales Assistants	Sales Manager
Payroll Assistant	Accounting Department Manager
Accounting Department Manager	General Manager

TASK 6

Match which ONE person each role must report to:

Role	Reports to
Accounts assistant	Payroll manager
Sales Ledger clerk	Finance Director
Machine operator	HR Manager
	Factory Manager
	Accounting department manager
	Marketing assistant

TASK 7

Select two actions that will ensure the legal compliance and two actions that will help the solvency of a business

Action	Legal Compliance	Solvency
Ensure financial statements are filed on time.		
Improve credit control procedures.		
Maintain a petty cash book.		
Create and maintain a cash budget.		
Ensure the work place is a safe environment for staff and visitors.		

TASK 8

The Accounting function is an essential part of the business. **Select two actions for each of the columns. Actions should only be selected once:**

Actions	Efficient running of the business	Solvency of the business	Legal Compliance
Monitor cashflow.			
Provide quotation to customer.			
Ensure Sales Tax is paid to HMRC on time			
Regularly chase outstanding receivables.			
Ensure inventory is ordered when it falls to the minimum level.			
Ensure members of staff are first aid trained.			
Regular maintenance of machinery.			
Produce a staff rota for tea making.			

LITERACY (EMAIL)

TASK 9

You are the manager of an accountancy firm (bob – bob@accountancyfirm.co.uk)

You want to discuss the exam performance of the AAT trainees with the training manager, Ally Mckoist (ally@accountancyfirm.co.uk). One student in particular (John Barnes) has performed poorly.

Please complete this email by selected from the drop down lists and filling the blanks:

From: bob@accountancyfirm.co.uk

To: _____

Subject: **(Hello/Discussion/AAT feedback/AAT Exam Performance)**

Hello Ally,

I would like to discuss the above with you **(now/whenever/tomorrow afternoon)**. In particular I would like to review the performance of **(Johnboy/Jimsy/John Barnes)** with a view to finding out why he has performed **(poorly/so well/good)**. I also hope we can resolve this issue by **(threatening John with the sack/working together with John/sending him an email)**.

Regards

Bob

TASK 10

Complete the e-mail shown below, which is confirming an appointment with a client Mr K Kipling (kk@cakes4tea.org.uk) to take place at his premises on Monday at 2.30 pm to discuss the business plan for the forthcoming year with Mrs Anna Howes.

From: AATstudent@Kaplan.co.uk

To: _____

Subject: **(Meeting request, meeting confirmation, telephone call)**

Good Morning Mr Kipling

Following our telephone conversation I confirm the meeting which is to take place at **(your home/ your premises/your bank)** on **(Saturday/Sunday/Monday/Tuesday)** at **(12.30 pm/1.30 pm/ 2 pm/2.30 pm/3 pm).**

I will bring a copy of the business plan I have prepared.

Kind regards

(Ann Howes

Anna How

Anna Howes)

TASK 11

The following is a partially completed email to inform Joshua Valentine (jvalentine@atoz.org.uk), Carmel Jenton (cjenton@atoz.org.uk) and Dane Wheeler (dwheeler@atoz.org.uk) of a conference on Thursday at 10am in the King's Hotel. The conference is being held to cover the issue of recycling within organisations. **Please complete as appropriate.**

From: AATstudent@atoz.org.uk

To: _____

_____

Subject:_____

Hello All,

This conference is being held at _____ on _____ at _____am.

The conference will be held regarding the issue of recycling within organisations.

Please confirm your attendance.

Regards,

AAT Student

PRIORITISATION OF WORK

TASK 12

Below is your work scheduled to be completed this week. You work part time from 8 am to 4 pm Monday to Wednesday and you have an hour for lunch at 12.30 pm. There is the weekly planning meeting on Monday at 8.15 am which lasts for 45 minutes.

You routine tasks for the week are:

Daily

Open and distribute the post	9 am (takes 1 hour)
Frank post and take to the post office	3.30 pm (takes 30 mins)

Monday

Process Sales invoices onto Sage	10 am (takes 1 hr 30 mins)

Tuesday

Process Purchase invoices onto Sage	10.30 pm (takes 1 hr 30 mins)

Wednesday

Prepare bank and petty cash reconciliations	1 hour

You have been requested to assist the Payroll Manager on Monday afternoon to calculate the Salesmen's bonuses for the period which must be processed on Tuesday at 2 pm to ensure these are paid at the end of the week.

Complete your to do list for Monday in order of task completion.

(1)

(2)

(3)

(4)

(5)

TASK 13

Your workload for the week is listed in the table below. Your hours of work are 9am to 5pm with an hour for lunch from 12pm to 1pm. There is a compulsory staff meeting on a Monday afternoon at 1pm, which lasts for one hour. You are required to take the minutes of this meeting.

Task	Task to be completed by:		Task Duration
	Day	Time	
Complete supplier payment run.	Thursday	11am	2 hours
Answer customer and supplier emails.	Daily	12pm	1 hour
Bank reconciliation.	Friday	5pm	2 hours
Process purchase invoices.	Tuesday	10am	3 hours
Process sales invoices.	Monday	12pm	2 hours
Prepare payment run information.	Wednesday	3pm	3 hours

Your manager has sent you the following email:

Hi,

I have been asked to prepare a report for senior management regarding the petty cash expenditure of the business, as it seems to be increasing quite dramatically. I require you to complete a petty cash reconciliation, which should take no longer than 1 hour to complete. My meeting is at 4pm on Monday afternoon and I require the information one hour prior.

Thank you

Complete a To-Do list for Monday in order of priority.

	First Task
	Second Task
	Third Task
	Fourth Task

TASK 14

Your workload for the coming week is shown below. You work from 9am to 5pm and take a lunch break from 12:30 – 1:30pm every day.

Task	Tasks to be completed by:		
	Day	*Time*	*Task Duration*
Process payroll.	Friday	11am	2 hrs
Bank reconciliations.	Every day	4.30pm	1 hr
Wages reconciliation.	Thursday	12pm	3 hrs
Overtime calculation.	Wednesday	12pm	2 hrs
Team meeting.	Thursday	10am	1 hr
Cash to bank.	Every day	5pm	½ hr

You receive the following email from your line manager on Wednesday at 5pm:

Hi,

Tomorrow I will be leaving the office at 2pm to meet a potential new customer. I will need to check the wages reconciliation before I go so that the staff are paid on Friday.

Thanks

Tomorrow is Thursday. Please list the order in which you are to complete these tasks:

Process payroll	(1st, 2nd, 3rd, 4th, 5th, 6th)
Bank reconciliation	(1st, 2nd, 3rd, 4th, 5th, 6th)
Wages reconciliation	(1st, 2nd, 3rd, 4th, 5th, 6th)
Overtime calculation	(1st, 2nd, 3rd, 4th, 5th, 6th)
Team meeting	(1st, 2nd, 3rd, 4th, 5th, 6th)
Cash to bank	(1st, 2nd, 3rd, 4th, 5th, 6th)

LITERACY (ERRORS)

TASK 15

This is a draft letter to be addressed to Mrs May, of MayMe Ltd, a supplier, regarding the incorrect amount being recorded on an invoice.

Review the letter and identify FIVE words which are spelled incorrectly, or are inappropriate.

Hi Mrs May,

Please find enclosed a copy of the invoice received from MayMe Ltd for a recent purchase.

The unit price stated on the invoice is incorrect. The unit price was quoted at £36 per unit on the purchase order, yet we have been invoiced £63 per unit.

Pleaze credit this invoice and reissue with the correct amount of £36 per unit. One we have received the corrected invoice, we can make payment.

Yours faithfully

TASK 16

Below is a response to a customer complaint. **Please highlight five words that are spelt incorrectly, or are Inappropriate:**

Dear Billy,

I was very cheesed to here that you did not receive your goods in proper working order. We have very strict internal procedures, which are designed to prevent faulty goods reaching our customers. Please rest assured that we are investigating fully you're case and are striving to ensure that this does not happen again in the future.

By way of an apolojy we will be refunding you in full and offering you a 20% discount off your next purchase.

Kind regards

John Anderson

Store manager

TASK 17

Review the draft correspondence below highlighting the spelling errors and inappropriate wording used.

Dear Mr Cadbury

I enclose a copy of the invoice which your requested during are telephone conversation this morning.

Please note this invoice is dated 31 June and therefor is overdue for payment.

I look forward to receiving your cheque in full settlement by return of post.

Yours faithfully

NUMERACY

TASK 18

Sales for the quarter.

Eastern region	£200,000
Western region	£180,000
South	£150,000
North	£160,000

(a)   What is the total sales figure for the quarter?

(b)   What percentage of the total sales was made by the North (round your answer to 2 decimal places)?

(c)   What percentage of total sales was made by the Eastern and Western regions (round your answer to 2 decimal places)?

TASK 19

Below are the sales figures for the first 6 months of Bradley Wiggins Limited (round answers to 2 decimal places).

Month	Sales – (£)
Month 1	456,123
Month 2	459,578
Month 3	461,591
Month 4	465,837
Month 5	468,149
Month 6	472,298

(a)   What are the total sales for the first 3 months?

(b)   What is the percentage increase from month 1 to month 2?

(c)   What will month 7 sales be if they are 5% higher than month 6?

(d)   How much higher (in £) are month 4 sales than month 2?

TASK 20

(a)   The following are the sales figures for an organisation for one year:

(Round your answers to 2 decimal places.)

Department	Sales – (£)
A	247,964
B	555,922
C	101,282
D	438,765

What is the total Sales figure for the year?

What percentage of total sales was made by Department B?

What percentage of total sales was made by Department A and D combined?

(b) **Using the above, complete the following statement.**

The total sales made by Department A and D are greater than/equal to/less than the total sales made by Departments B and C.

PERSONAL DEVELOPMENT

TASK 21

(a) **Identify two of the following activities that count towards an employee's Continuing Professional Development requirements.**

- Attend a client lunch meeting to discuss improving services offered.
- Complete a course to further relevant knowledge.
- Arrive at work one hour earlier every day during busy times.
- Read articles online related to the trade in which the employee works.

(b) **Identify the Strength, Weakness, Opportunity and Threat from the information listed below.**

	Strength	Weakness	Opportunity	Threat
Attend a time management course.				
Leaves filing to the end of the week.				
Excellent customer service.				
Insufficient staff members to cover time off for courses.				

TASK 22

Your manager has reviewed your performance over the past 6 months and the following has been noted.

Strengths	Weaknesses
Excellent computer skills.	Lack of confidence with clients .
Enthusiasm for learning.	Little double entry knowledge.

Indicate which courses would be appropriate for you to attend:

- Bookkeeping course.
- Online computer studies course.
- Communication and presentation skills.
- Nail art evening classes.
- Kick boxing classes.

Show whether the following statements are TRUE or FALSE.

A qualified accountant does not need to attend Continued Professional Development courses – True/False

CPD must be undertaken for a minimum of 1 day per month – True/False

TASK 23

(a) Your manager has assessed that you have the following weaknesses:

   (1) Poor communications skills.

   (2) Poor timekeeping.

   (3) Inadequate technical accounting skills.

   Which of the following 3 courses of action could address each of these?

   - Attend a bookkeeping course.
   - Learn to drive.
   - Buy new accounting software.
   - Adopt a new clock in and out system for the office.
   - Attend a 'how to communicate in an office' course.
   - Go on a sky dive course.

(b) **Please answer TRUE or FALSE.**

   All accountants, qualified and unqualified must complete CPD – True/False

   CPD must be carried out on an annual basis by unqualified members – True/False

   CPD must be carried out on an annual basis by qualified members – True/False

LITERACY (REPORT)

TASK 24

50 feedback forms have been sent out by e-mail to the delegates following a training course. The results are shown in the table below:

	Response	
Question	Yes	No
Was the course content relevant to your job role?	15	5
Did the presenter explain the purpose of the training?	20	1
Would you recommend the course to others?	18	2
Was the venue easy to find?	6	15

Select two conclusions that could be made from the feedback:

- The course was not relevant to the delegates job role.
- Most delegates found the venue difficult to find.
- The course was not very successful.
- The course was relevant to the delegates job role.

Select two items from the below list which are to be investigated:

- Why did we send the staff on the course?
- Why was there so little feedback received?
- Look for a different venue.
- Do we need to use a different presenter?

TASK 25

The following survey was recently carried out at a company.

	Number of staff that agreed	Number of staff that disagreed	Number of staff that did not answer
Are you happy with your work / life balance?	12	45	3
Are you satisfied with your current pay?	34	24	2
Do you believe you have strong promotion prospects in your current role?	5	55	0

(a)   How many people were asked each question?

(b)   In terms of work/life balance, are staff happy/unhappy?

(c)   In terms of current pay/are most people happy/unhappy?

(d)   Do the majority of people agree that there are good promotion prospects – yes/no?

TASK 26

What information is usually contained within the areas of a report listed below?

	Introduction	Appendices
Information regarding what the report is based upon.		
Supporting calculations for figures contained within the body of the report.		

IMPACT OF WORK ON OTHERS

TASK 27

Some issues should be referred to a manager if they are unable to be resolved easily by an employee.

Which TWO of the following issues would you try to resolve yourself?

- The paper for the photocopier keeps running out without a new order being placed.
- You suspect a colleague is being harassed by another colleague.
- Your manager has requested you complete a task you do not have sufficient knowledge to complete.
- Somebody in the office continues to prop the fire door open.

TASK 28

Identify the most likely effect on the organisation if you were unable to complete the petty cash reconciliation on time.

- Your colleagues would be unable to complete their work on time.
- Fraudulent activity may have taken place and go undetected.
- Petty cash will be withdrawn, replaced with invoicing for small purchases.

TASK 29

Some issues may lead to conflict in the workplace. **Indicate which issues can be resolved by you and which should be referred to your line manager.**

Issue	Resolve myself	Refer to line manager
Your manager has asked you to complete a Statement of Financial position; however you do not have the accounting knowledge to do this.		
You suspect your colleague knows your computer password.		
You suspect an expenses form which has been passed to you has non-business expenses on it and the form has been submitted by a manager.		

ETHICAL VALUES AND PRINCIPLES

TASK 30

The fundamental code of Ethics set out five principles that a professional accountant is required to comply with. Two principles are objectivity and professional competence/due care. **From the list select two others.**

A   Confidence.

B   Integrity.

C   Truthfulness.

D   Confidentiality.

TASK 31

Your father owns some shares in a company which your company audits. You have recently found out that the company is struggling. This is going to be announced publicly shortly and will have an adverse effect on the share price. **Which TWO fundamental principles prevent you from telling your father about this?**

A   Confidentiality.

B   Objectivity.

C   Professional Behaviour.

D   Professional competence and due care.

E   Integrity

TASK 32

Your best friend has recently started up in business and really needs some tax advice. Because they know you are training to be an accountant they have automatically assumed you are the right person to give advice. **Which fundamental principle prevents you from advising your best friend particularly regarding the fact that it is tax advice that he is seeking?**

A   Confidentiality.

B   Objectivity.

C   Professional Behaviour.

D   Professional competence and due care.

E   Integrity.

TASK 33

You and a work colleague decide to go out for dinner after work. Whilst in the restaurant you start to discuss a client and the issues which this client is currently facing. Unbeknown to you the CEO of their major supplier is sat at the next table and hears everything which you have discussed. **Which fundamental code of ethics prevents you and your colleague from discussing this in public?**

A   Confidentiality.

B   Objectivity.

C   Professional Behaviour.

D   Professional competence and due care.

E   Integrity.

TASK 34

Your work colleague has decided not to comply with the relevant accounting legislation when preparing a client's account as they 'can't be bothered'. **Which two fundamental principles is your colleague in breach of?**

A   Confidentiality.

B   Objectivity.

C   Professional Behaviour.

D   Professional competence and due care.

E   Integrity.

TASK 35

You have recently discovered that your manager is committing fraud. Your manager suspects that you know, and have threatened you with termination of your contract if you decide to whistle blow him. **Which threat to principles are you being faced with?**

A   Self Interest.

B   Self Review.

C   Familiarity.

D   Advocacy.

E   Intimidation.

TASK 36

Your company has recently taken on a new client and you have been asked to prepare the monthly management accounts. As soon as you start work on the accounts you realise that it is your Auntie's Company. **Which threat to principles are you being faced with?**

A   Self Interest.

B   Self Review.

C   Familiarity.

D   Advocacy.

E   Intimidation.

SUSTAINABLE INITIATIVES AND BENEFITS

TASK 37

What do the 3 Ps relate to in terms of balancing economic, environment and social needs?

A   People, Planet, Product.

B   Planet, Place, Product.

C   Profit, People, Planet.

D   Price, People, Product.

E   Profit, Place, People.

TASK 38

Kaplan Financial is looking to become more sustainable and the AAT National Product Manager believes that she has come up with a few amazing suggestions. **Which one of these suggestions actually relates to sustainability?**

A   Encourage all staff and students to use their own cars to travel to and from Kaplan.

B   Ensure all lights and computers are left on in the evening to prevent break-ins.

C   Encourage all students and staff to throw paper in the normal waste bin.

D   Encourage all AAT Kaplan staff to work through their lunch.

E   To look into the possibility of providing the AAT textbook via e-books instead of providing a paper copy to students.

TASK 39

Your friend is being encouraged to make a suggestion of how to improve sustainability within her workplace. Which one of these suggestions should she put forward to her manager?

A   Encourage all staff to print their work and maintain in lever arch files for audit trail purposes.

B   Look at installing motion sensor lights into the office block.

C   Encourage the Financial Accountant to replace his 2.0L Diesel BMW with a 3.5L Petrol BMW.

D   Suggest that all Monthly regional meetings should be done in the most central regional office.

E   Ensure all trainee accountants complete their CPD.

TASK 40

A company is looking to improve sustainability and it has been looking at installing solar panels on the office roof to reduce their yearly electricity costs. However the initial costs of implementing this is 20% higher than originally budgeted for. **Should the company still pursue this even though it is going to have an adverse impact on cost?**

A   Yes

B   No

Section 2

ANSWERS TO PRACTICE QUESTIONS

ACCOUNTING FUNCTION, POLICIES AND PROCEDURES

TASK 1

Select three of the following policies and procedures which are likely to apply to the accounting function:

A   **Data Protection Act**

B   **Health and Safety at Work**

D   **Authorised Signatory Procedure**

TASK 2

Various documents are provided to the accounts department, match the document to the department sending it:

Department	Document
Purchasing Department	**(b) Copy of Purchase order**
HR Department	**(d) New employee forms**
Payroll Department	**(e) Statutory Sick pay forms**

TASK 3

Match the following departments to **one** information type

Department	Information
Sales Dept	**Commission payable to sales staff**
Accounts Dept	**Cheque book stubs**
Payroll Dept	**List of all new employees for period**

TASK 4

Select THREE principles from the list below that are not part of the Data Protection Act 1998.

- **Information obtained for personal use**

- **Historic information that is not up to date**

- **Transferred to other countries without authorisation**

REPORTING LINES AND CONTRIBUTIONS OF PEOPLE AND FUNCTIONS

TASK 5

A business employs 2 Directors, 3 Managers and 6 Assistants. State who should report to who.

Sales and Purchase Ledger Assistant	**Accounting Department Manager**
Administration Assistant	**General Manager**
3 Sales Assistants	**Sales Manager**
Payroll Assistant	**Accounting Department Manager**
Accounting Department Manager	**Financial Director**

TASK 6

Match which **one** person each role must report to:

Role	Reports to
Accounts assistant	**Accounting department manager**
Sales Ledger clerk	**Accounting department manager**
Machine operator	**Factory Manager**

TASK 7

Select two actions that will ensure the legal compliance and two actions that will help the solvency of a business

Action	Legal Compliance	Solvency
Ensure financial statements are filed on time	✓	
Improve credit control procedures		✓
Maintain a petty cash book		
Create and maintain a cash budget		✓
Ensure the work place is a safe environment for staff and visitors	✓	

TASK 8

The Accounting function is an essential part of the business. Select two actions for each of the columns. Actions should only be selected once:

Actions	Efficient running of the business	Solvency of the business	Legal Compliance
Monitor cashflow		✓	
Provide quotation to customer			
Ensure Sales Tax is paid to HMRC on time			✓
Regularly chase outstanding receivables		✓	
Ensure inventory is ordered when it falls to the minimum level	✓		
Ensure members of staff are first aid trained			✓
Regular maintenance of machinery	✓		
Produce a staff rota for tea making			

LITERACY (EMAIL)

TASK 9

From: bob@accountancyfirm.co.uk

To: ally@accountancyfirm.co.uk

Subject: **AAT Exam Performance**

Hello Ally,

I would like to discuss the above with you **tomorrow afternoon**. In particular I would like to review the performance of **John Barnes** with a view to finding out why he has performed **poorly**. I also hope we can resolve this issue by **working together with John**.

Regards

Bob

TASK 10

From AATstudent@Kaplan.co.uk

To: kk@cakes4tea.org.uk

Subject: **Meeting confirmation**

Good morning Mr Kipling

Following our telephone conversation I confirm the meeting which is to take place at **your premises**, on **Monday** at **2.30 pm**.

I will bring a copy of the business plan I have prepared.

Kind regards

Anna Howes

TASK 11

From: AATstudent@atoz.org.uk

To: jvalentine@atoz.org.uk; cjenton@atoz.org.uk; dwheeler@atoz.org.uk

Subject: **Conference**

Hello All,

This conference is being held at **King's Hotel** on **Thursday** at **10** am.

The conference will be held regarding the issue of recycling within organisations.

Please confirm your attendance.

Regards,

AAT Student

PRIORITISATION OF WORK

TASK 12

Complete your to do list for Monday in order of task completion.

(1)   **Weekly planning meeting**

(2)   **Open and distribute post**

(3)   **Process sales invoices**

(4)   **Assist payroll manager**

(5)   **Frank post and take to PO**

TASK 13

Complete a To-Do list for Monday in order of priority.

Answer customer and supplier emails	First Task
Process sales invoices	Second Task
Staff meeting	Third Task
Petty cash reconciliation	Fourth Task

TASK 14

Process payroll	5th
Bank reconciliation	3rd
Wages reconciliation	2nd
Overtime calculation	6th
Team meeting	1st
Cash to bank	4th

LITERACY (ERRORS)

TASK 15

Hi Mrs May,

Please find enclosed a copy of the invoice received from MayMe Ltd for a recent purchase.

The unit price stated on the invoice is incorrect. The unit price **wos** quoted at £36 per unit on the purchase order, yet we have been invoiced £63 per unit.

Pleaze credit this invoice and reissue with the correct amount of £36 per unit. **One** we have received the corrected invoice, we can make payment.

Yours **faithfully**

TASK 16

Dear **Billy**,

I was very **cheesed** to **here** that you did not receive your goods in proper working order. We have very strict internal procedures, which are designed to prevent faulty goods reaching our customers. Please rest assured that we are investigating fully **you're** case and are striving to ensure that this does not happen again in the future.

By way of an **apolojy** we will be refunding you in full and offering you a 20% discount on your next purchase,

Kind regards

John Anderson

Store manager

TASK 17

Dear Mr Cadbury

I enclose a copy of the invoice which **your** requested during **are** telephone conversation this morning.

Please note this invoice is dated **31** June and **therefor** is overdue for payment.

I look forward to receiving your cheque in full settlement by return of post.

Yours **faithfully**

NUMERACY

TASK 18

(a)   What is the total sales figure for the quarter?   **£690,000**

(b)   What percentage of the total sales was made by the North (round your answer to 2 decimal places)?   **23.19%**

(c)   What percentage of total sales was made by the Eastern and Western regions (round your answer to 2 decimal places)?   **55.07%**

TASK 19

(a)   What are the total sales for the first 3 months?   **£1,377,292**

(b)   What is the percentage increase from month 1 to month 2?   **0.76%**

(c)   What will month 7 sales be if they are 5% higher than month 6?   **£495,912.90**

(d)   How much higher (in £) are month 4 sales than month 2?   **£6,259**

TASK 20

(a)   What is the total Sales figure for the year?

£1,343,933

What percentage of total sales was made by Department B?

41.37%

What percentage of total sales was made by Department A and D combined?

51.10%

(b)   Using the above, complete the following statement.

The total sales made by Department A and D are **greater than** the total sales made by Departments B and C.

PERSONAL DEVELOPMENT

TASK 21

(a)   Identify two of the following activities that count towards an employee's continuing professional development requirements.

- **Complete a course to further relevant knowledge**

- **Read articles online related to the trade in which the employee works**

(b)   Identify the strength, weakness, opportunity and threat from the information listed below.

	Strength	Weakness	Opportunity	Threat
Attend a time management course			✓	
Leaves filing to the end of the week		✓		
Excellent customer service	✓			
Insufficient staff members to cover time off for courses				✓

TASK 22

Indicate which courses would be appropriate for you to attend:

- **Bookkeeping course**

- **Communication and presentation skills**

Show whether the following statements are TRUE or FALSE.

A qualified accountant does not need to attend Continued Professional Development courses – **False**

CPD must be undertaken for a minimum of 1 day per month – **False**

TASK 23

(a)   Your manager has assessed that you have the following weaknesses:

   (1)   Poor communications skills – **Attend a 'how to communicate in an office' course**

   (2)   Poor timekeeping – **Adopt a new clock in and out system for the office**

   (3)   Inadequate technical accounting skills – **Attend a bookkeeping course**

(b)   Please answer TRUE or FALSE

   All accountants, qualified and unqualified must complete CPD – **False**

   CPD must be carried out on an annual basis by unqualified members – **False**

   CPD must be carried out on an annual basis by qualified members – **True**

LITERACY (REPORT)

TASK 24

Select two conclusions that could be made from the feedback

- **Most delegates found the venue difficult to find**
- **The course was relevant to the delegates job role**

Select two items from the below list which are to be investigated

- **Why was there so little feedback received**
- **Look for a different venue**

TASK 25

(a)   How many people were asked each question? **60**

(b)   In terms of work/life balance, are staff **unhappy**

(c)   In terms of current pay/ are most people **happy**

(d)   Do the majority of people agree that there are good promotion prospects – **no**

TASK 26

What information is usually contained within the areas of a report listed below?

	Introduction	Appendices
Information regarding what the report is based upon	✓	
Supporting calculations for figures contained within the body of the report		✓

IMPACT OF WORK ON OTHERS

TASK 27

Which TWO of the following issues would you try to resolve yourself?

- **The paper for the photocopier keeps running out without a new order being placed.**
- **Somebody in the office continues to prop the fire door open.**

TASK 28

Identify the most likely effect on the organisation if you were unable to complete the petty cash reconciliation on time.

- **Fraudulent activity may have taken place and go undetected**

TASK 29

Some issues may lead to conflict in the workplace. Indicate which issues can be resolved by you and which should be referred to your line manager.

Issue	Resolve myself	Refer to line manager
Your manager has asked you to complete a Statement of Financial position, however you do not have the accounting knowledge to do this		✓
You suspect your colleague knows your computer password	✓	
You suspect an expenses form which has been passed to you has non-business expenses on it and the form has been submitted by a manager		✓

ETHICAL VALUES AND PRINCIPLES

TASK 30

The fundamental code of Ethics set out five principles that a professional accountant is required to comply with. Two principles are objectivity and professional competence/due care. From the list select two others?

B   **Integrity**

D   **Confidentiality**

TASK 31

Your father owns some shares in a company which your company audits. You have recently found out that the company is struggling. This is going to be announced publicly shortly and will have an adverse effect on the share price. Which two fundamental principles prevents you from telling your father about this?

A   **Confidentiality**

B   **Objectivity**

TASK 32

Your best friend has recently started up in business and really needs some tax advice. Because they know you are training to be an accountant they have automatically assumed you are the right person to give advice. Which fundamental principle prevents you from advising your best friend particularly regarding the fact that it is tax advice that he is seeking?

D   **Professional competence and due care**

TASK 33

You and a work colleague decide to go out for dinner after work. Whilst in the restaurant you start to discuss a client and the issues which this client is currently facing. Unbeknown to you the CEO of their major supplier is sat at the next table and hears everything which you have discussed. Which fundamental code of ethics prevents you and your colleague from discussing this in public?

A   **Confidentiality**

TASK 34

Your work colleague has decided not to comply with the relevant accounting legislation when preparing a client's account as they 'can't be bothered'. Which two fundamental principles is your colleague in breach of?

C   **Professional Behaviour**

D   **Professional competence and due care**

TASK 35

You have recently discovered that your manager is committing fraud. Your manager suspects that you know, and have threatened you with termination of your contract if you decide to whistle blow him. Which threat to principles are you being faced with?

E   **Intimidation**

TASK 36

Your company has recently taken on a new client and you have been asked to prepare the monthly management accounts. As soon as you start work on the accounts you realise that it is your Auntie's Company. Which threat to principles are you being faced with?

C   **Familiarity**

SUSTAINABLE INITIATIVES AND BENEFITS

TASK 37

What do the 3 Ps relate to in terms of balancing economic, environment and social needs?

C   **Profit, People, Planet**

TASK 38

Kaplan Financial is looking to become more sustainable and the AAT National Product Manager believes that she has come up with a few amazing suggestions. Which one of these suggestions actually relates to sustainability?

E   **To look into the possibility of providing the AAT textbook via e-books instead of providing a paper copy to students**

TASK 39

Your friend is being encouraged to make a suggestion of how to improve sustainability within her workplace. Which one of these suggestions should she put forward to her manager?

B   **Look at installing motion sensor lights into the office block**

TASK 40

A company is looking to improve sustainability and it has been looking at installing solar panels on the office roof to reduce their yearly electricity costs. However the initial costs of implementing this is 20% higher than originally budgeted for. Should the company still pursue this even though it is going to have an adverse impact on cost?

A   **Yes**